Noodle Doodle Box

Adapted and Translated by
Anita and Alex Page

A SAMUEL FRENCH ACTING EDITION

SAMUEL FRENCH

FOUNDED 1830

SAMUELFRENCH.COM
SAMUELFRENCH-LONDON.CO.UK

Please refer to page 35 for further copyright information.

CAST OF CHARACTERS

Written For a Flexible Cast of Three,
3M, 3F or Mixed Cast

ZACHARIAS, *the big, strong one. He wears a jacket with a wide plaid design, shoulders excessively padded, and underneath a striped pullover. His pants are too short and too tight. In addition, he wears laced boots and a bowler hat.*

PEPPER, *the little one. His pants are far too big and he has them pulled up by suspenders, almost to his armpits. They are still too long. On top of them, he wears a tuxedo jacket that's much too small for him and which is held together in front with a safety pin. His sleeves stop above the elbows. He almost always walks around in stocking feet.*

THE DRUM MAJOR *may be white-faced. He has on a fantastic uniform with gaudy decorations hanging from it. On his chest medals clang, and his cap has colorful little windmills which turn as he walks. A large marching drum hangs from his neck. On top of the drum is a cymbal. Maybe there are even colored bulbs on his shoulders which light up when he marches.*

NOTES ON THE PRODUCTION

The major set pieces for *Noodle Doodle Box* are two wooden boxes, large enough for an adult actor to disappear into, screens or a pair of hinged flats to serve as a backdrop, and a variety of different-sized cardboard boxes and cartons. The simplicity of the setting makes it ideal for touring.

ZACHARIAS' box, the smaller of the two wooden ones, is painted red on two adjoining sides and green on the remaining ones. It should be placed on stage so that only two sides of the same color are seen by the audience. PEPPER's box, the larger one, has two holes on opposite sides, the holes large enough to put an arm through. Attached to the inside of the box, next to each hole, are a large cardboard arm on the right and a doll's arm on the left. Each of them is pushed through a hole by Pepper on page 13. The doll's arm should be the same color as Pepper's jacket sleeve.

The cardboard boxes and cartons remain behind the backdrop until page 29 when ZACHARIAS goes behind it several times, "magically," returning to the playing area each time using a larger box than the one he began with.

PEPPER and ZACHARIAS' costumes suggest certain clown types but the two should not be played in a broad slapstick manner, rather with a subtle suggestion of those stock characters. Hopefully, the full stage directions will serve the actor and director as suggestions for imaginative stage action and movement and not as constraints.

In keeping with the spontaneity with which ZACHARIAS and PEPPER sing, the music for the songs in this script are left to the improvisation of the actors.

4

Noodle Doodle Box

SETTING: *The stage is empty. In the* CENTER, *however, there are two large different-colored boxes; one is a little larger than the other.*

AT RISE: *For a while, nothing happens. Then a cock crows loudly: cock-a-doodle-doo.* ZACHARIAS *appears out of the smaller box. Leisurely he takes his toothbrush from his pocket and brushes his teeth. Then he takes off his hat and brushes his hair with the toothbrush. He puts on his hat, disappears into the box and now reappears with one black and one white shoe. Now he brushes the shoe with his toothbrush. Meantime out of the other box rises* PEPPER. *His hair is all uncombed. He yawns, stretches, and then starts to do kneebends. His head slowly disappears inside the box with each bend and then he rises up again.*

ZACHARIAS. Pepper!
PEPPER. (*Stops his exercises. His head comes up just beyond the edge of the box*) Yes?
ZACH. You're a pig! (*He spits on his toothbrush and keeps brushing his shoes*)
PEPPER. Indeed! (*He contines his kneebends but speeds them up*)
ZACH. (*Stops cleaning his shoes. Interested, he watches* PEPPER *doing his kneebends. His head keeps time with* PEPPER. *He stops and yells*) Pepper!
PEPPER. (*He stops in the middle of moving*) Yes?
ZACH. Don't you want to know why you are one?
PEPPER. One what?
ZACH. A pig.
PEPPER. (*Gently*) Yes, Zacky. You can tell me.

5

ZACH. How many times do I have to tell you that my name is Zach-a-ri-as.

PEPPER. Your name is too long. (*Assuredly*) Names that are too long can be shortened.

ZACH. Nothing is going to be shortened. I don't call you Pep.

PEPPER. You may call me Pep. I don't like Pepper anyway.

ZACH. (*Laughs smugly*) Every person has the name that he deserves. (*He speaks grandly*) Zach-a-ri-as! (*Then briefly and sharply*) Pepper! (*He spits contemptuously on his shoes and continues to clean them*)

PEPPER. (*After thinking briefly*) Listen, Zack.

ZACH. Zacharias, you ass!

PEPPER. (*Unshaken*) Listen, Zachariassss.

ZACH. What?

PEPPER. You were going to tell me why I am one.

ZACH. One what?

PEPPER. A piglet?

ZACH. Oh, yes, of course. You are a pig because you don't take care of yourself. Look at me; brushed my teeth, combed my hair, shined my shoes.

　　A sloppy Joe is not quite okay;
　　Big shots wash nearly every day.

PEPPER. Hey, Zacharias.

ZACH. What?

PEPPER. You've got strange shoes. One is black and one is white.

ZACH. (*Inspects them attentively*) That's curious.

PEPPER. What does that mean?

ZACH. That's funny. That's even more curious.

PEPPER. What is it?

ZACH. Even more curiouser. Because here in the box, I actually have another pair like that. (*He holds the second pair of shoes up high*)

PEPPER. There has to be a shoe sickness.

ZACH. (*Worried*) You think so?

PEPPER. Maybe it's contagious. (*He descends into his box and rises with two huge black shoes. Triumphantly*) My shoes haven't caught it yet. Don't come too close with yours, Zacky.

ZACH. (*Correcting him*) . . . ariasssssss!

PEPPER. (*Thinking he is supposed to speak more quietly, whispers*) Not too close, Zachary.

ZACH. (*Angrily and emphatically*) sss ssss ssss!

PEPPER. (*Looks around anxiously and whispers*) Don't be afraid. I won't tell anybody that you have infected shoes, Zacky.

ZACH. (*Throws all four shoes furiously to the ground in front of the box*) Zacharias, you camel! Zacharias!

PEPPER. Today, you aren't being very nice to me. You just said I'm a camel. I don't think I like that.

ZACH. Don't start blubbering. Help me out of the box.

PEPPER. Okay, Zacharias. (*He climbs out of his box and runs in stocking feet to the other box. En route he stumbles over the shoes which* ZACHARIAS *had thrown out earlier and pushes them instinctively together so that two black and two white shoes make two pairs next to each other. Then he slowly pulls up bulky* ZACHARIAS)

ZACH. Careful. Not so fast.

PEPPER. (*He has almost pulled* ZACHARIAS *out of the box when he suddenly realizes that the correct pairs are lined up. Bewildered, he lets go of him.* ZACHARIAS *falls back into the box with a loud racket.* PEPPER *inspects the shoes from close up, quite untroubled*) Hey, Zacky.

ZACH. (*Corrrects* PEPPER, *his voice muffled from inside the box*) Zachariasss.

PEPPER. Hey, Zachariasss. Look at those shoes. They're healthy again.

ZACH. (*Wide-eyed, looks over the edge of the box*) So it is. Fantastomatic.

PEPPER. I even know what made them healthy. The nose dive is what healed them. That's what I'm going to write in all the newspapers. "Pepper's cure for sick shoes, works triple A one, okay and quick."

ZACH. Don't talk such nonsense.

PEPPER. What?

ZACH. You don't even know how to write.

PEPPER. But I can read.

ZACH. So you can read! Then read something that's in the newspaper. (*He gets a newspaper out of the box and holds it in front of* PEPPER)

PEPPER. (PEPPER *holds it upside down, opens it and mumbles to show that he is earnestly "reading"*) Hum, hm, mhm.

ZACH. (*Climbs out of his box and looks with interest over* PEPPER's *shoulder, happily surprised*) Read it louder!

PEPPER. (*Pushes him back a couple of steps and assumes a grand posture.* ZACHARIAS *waits patiently in amazement.* PEPPER *reads with expressive head movements and large gestures*)

> Two frogs went on a Friday
> To the barber in the Mall
> For the very latest hairdo

(*Noisily turns the page*)

> For a very important ball.
> The barber looked and cried:
> My, what a silly pair
> To ask for a fancy hairdo

(*Turns the page*)

> And you don't have a single hair!

(*At first* ZACHARIAS *has listened attentively, moving his head in time to the rhythm of the lines. Suddenly he stops; his glance stays glued to the front page, he lowers his head and looks at it from closer up. Then he walks around* PEPPER, *looks over his shoulder as he is reading and waits, furious, until he is finished.* PEPPER *turns around and looks proudly at him.* ZACHARIAS *very calmly takes the paper from* PEPPER's *hands, folds it carefully together several times and hits* PEPPER *over the head with it*) You, phony! (*Hits him*) You deceiver! (*Hits him again*) You, show-off! (*Hits him*) You big mouth! (*Hits him twice*) You can't read at all. You've said everything by heart. The newspaper is upside down. I could tell by the pictures!

PEPPER. (*Crying*) You're mean. All day you've been bawling me out. First, I'm a pig, then a donkey, then a camel, then a big louse.

ZACH. Big louse! Big mouth I said and that's what you are. (PEPPER *cries louder*) Well, a small mouth. (PEPPER *keeps on crying*) A mini mouth.

PEPPER. And you've been hitting me too!

ZACH. But only with paper.

PEPPER. Hitting, all the same. I'm not going to be your friend any longer.

ZACH. Don't be so easy to insult. I'm going to give you a present.

PEPPER. (*Asks immediately, very businesslike*) What is it?

ZACH. My handkerchief. You can use it to wipe the tears away. (*He pulls out an immense handkerchief full of holes and passes it to* PEPPER. *He takes it and thrusts a finger through one of the holes and shakes his head. Finally, he folds it and wipes away his tears. But the holes bother him. He resumes crying*)

ZACH. Why are you bawling again?

PEPPER. Your handkerchief has holes.

ZACH. Holes? Where?

PEPPER. Here.

ZACH. All you have to do is turn the hanky around.

PEPPER. (*Pleased, turns the handkerchief around. But his face saddens again*) Here are also holes.

ZACH. Such a peculiar coincidence. Holes in back and holes in front.

PEPPER. That's the way it always is.

ZACH. What's always so?

PEPPER. Everything looks from behind exactly the way it looks from in front.

ZACH. What nonsense!

PEPPER. Here you go again—fighting.

ZACH. Naturally, if you say such nonsense. Since when are things the same in front as in back. I'm going to prove to you that you look different from behind than from in front. Stand there. (*He positions* PEPPER *facing the audience*) And now tell me what you see.

PEPPER. (*Looks at the audience. Shrugs his shoulders*) Children.

ZACH. No, no, no! You're supposed to look at yourself, your front. What do you see there?

PEPPER. One button, another button, a tummy, two legs and two socks.

ZACH. (*Nods in agreement. Then he turns* PEPPER *around so that his back faces the audience. Triumphant*) Are you going to claim that you look from behind exactly as in front? Then tell me what you see now?

PEPPER. A button, another button, a tummy, two legs, two socks.

ZACH. Oh, you . . . (*Furious, he throws his handkerchief at* PEPPER. PEPPER *walks away hurt*) Pepper!

PEPPER. (*Walks away, paying no attention.* ZACHARIAS *runs after him and holds him by his coat*)

ZACH. (*Flatteringly*) I just want to show you something. Don't be hurt, little Pepper.

PEPPER. Show! (*Contemptuously*) You just want to laugh at me. Show me how it works on your box.

ZACH. What?

PEPPER. That with a front and a back.

ZACH. Won't work.

PEPPER. Aha, won't work.

ZACH. Because it's too heavy.

PEPPER. Excuses, excuses.

ZACH. No . . .

PEPPER. Yes.

ZACH. No.

PEPPER. Then turn the box around.

ZACH. Okay. Let's turn it on my side.

PEPPER. No, on my side.

ZACH. No.

PEPPER. Okay, your side.

ZACH. Let's go. Let's turn it around. Push! (ZACHARIAS *takes a smaller box out of his larger one and puts it on the floor; then together they grab the large box, raise it and turn it around. Suddenly the green box is red.* ZACHARIAS *and* PEPPER *stare at it speechlessly.* ZACHARIAS *is even more astonished by the new color than* PEPPER)

ZACH. Did you see? First it was green. Now it's red.

PEPPER. Fabulous.

ZACH. Fantastomatic.

PEPPER. Super, now let's turn my box around.

ZACH. Okay. Let's turn your box around. What are those funny holes on the side?

PEPPER. I sawed them in.

ZACH. What for?

PEPPER. So I can put out my hand and find out if it's raining.

ZACH. Such foolishness! (PEPPER *bends over the edge of the box and pulls out all kinds of things: shoes, assorted objects, a half-filled water bottle. He gives it all to* ZACHARIAS, *who makes a small pile of them. When an object pleases him especially, he polishes it with his sleeve and lets it disappear in his pocket. Then both grab hold of the box and turn it. This one doesn't change color*)

PEPPER. Let's try again. (*They turn it over once again and again nothing changes*)

ZACH. Foolish box.

PEPPER. Dummy! (*He kicks the box angrily*)

ZACH. (*Standing before his box*) Now there's a box. Come, we'll turn it around. (*They turn the box*) You see? Green. (*They turn the box again*) And now, red. That's big-time stuff. Fantastomatic.

PEPPER. Zacky.

ZACH. Zachariasss.

PEPPER. Zacharias, won't you give me your box?

ZACH. Have you a screw loose in your head?

PEPPER. Can we swap? Mine is bigger. (*Zacharias points to his head, indicating that* PEPPER *is crazy*)

PEPPER. Will you lend it to me?

ZACH. (*Picking up the handkerchief and wiping invisible spots from the box*) A box isn't a rental car.

PEPPER. But I can step into it.

ZACH. With those dirty feet?!

PEPPER. I can put on my shoes.

ZACH. They haven't been cleaned.

PEPPER. If you don't let me in, I'm going to be really hurt. (ZACHARIAS *won't have it. He spits on his hanky and energetically polishes the box*) I'm going to find myself another friend.

ZACH. (*Still polishing. Offhand*) With that box? (*He

pulls his toothbrush out of his pocket and proceeds to clean the box with it)

PEPPER. I was kidding.

ZACH. (*Polishing*) Sounded quite serious.

PEPPER. I was really just kidding, Zacharias.

ZACH. That kind of kidding I don't find at all funny.

PEPPER. You're right, Zacharias. It was silly kidding. You can do better than that. Pretend you're the fountain, like yesterday; that was lots of fun.

ZACH. For that, I must put on my shoes.

PEPPER. Let me get them for you, Zacharias. The black or the white?

ZACH. The white, naturally, idiot.

PEPPER. (*Hurries to get the shoes. ZACHARIAS raises his leg. PEPPER bends down and puts the shoes on ZACHARIAS)* And now we'll play fountain together, okay?

ZACH. Together won't do because only one can play fountain.

PEPPER. You may play fountain. I'll get the water.

ZACH. There is no water.

PEPPER. Yes, there is, a whole bottle half full. (*He gets the water bottle*) I'll find a bucket.

ZACH. We don't need a bucket.

PEPPER. No bucket?

ZACH. Today we play an automatic fountain with electricity.

PEPPER. How does that work?

ZACH. You stand in front of the fountain. You say, please, water, please.

PEPPER. And then?

ZACH. Then you get some.

PEPPER. Where do I get it?

ZACH. You'll see.

PEPPER. Okay. Please, water, please.

ZACH. Wait. Not so fast. You have to go off a little way and then you come back and say it.

PEPPER. (*Eagerly takes a few steps. ZACHARIAS is about to fill his mouth with water. Just as he raises the bottle, PEPPER turns around and asks*) Like this?

(ZACHARIAS *quickly hides the bottle behind his back, accidentally pouring water over his coat. He sup-*

presses his anger. He says in a kindly way) No, a
bit further. (*While* PEPPER *goes off further, he angrily shakes off the spilled water. He again raises the
bottle.* PEPPER *turns around a second time.* ZACH-
ARIAS *hides the bottle and again wets the jacket*)

PEPPER. Should I come?

ZACH. Don't ask every three steps whether you should
come or not. Go on, further.

PEPPER. Okay, Zacharias, I'm going.

ZACH. (*Fills his mouth with water and stands waiting
with full cheeks.* PEPPER *continues to walk and disappears* OFF-STAGE. ZACHARIAS *keeps waiting, bangs his foot
on the floor impatiently. At last, he spits out the water in
a high arc and yells*) Pepper!

PEPPER. (*Comes running happily*) Please, water, please.

ZACH. No, no, no. You do it all wrong. Let's do it over.
Now you take ten paces, turn around and come back here
to me. Got it?

PEPPER. Got it, Zacharias. One, two, three, four, six,
five, eight, ten. Coming. (ZACHARIAS *has his mouth full
of water.* PEPPER *stops in front of* ZACHARIAS, *looks at
him questioningly.* ZACHARIAS *nods graciously*) Please,
water, please.

ZACH. (*Sprays the water into his face. He almost falls
over from laughing so hard. He keeps thumping* PEPPER
on his shoulder) Ho, ho, ho. That was some kidding, eh?
Fantastomatic. Lots of fun. You should have seen your
face when the water hit you—like a worm in a puddle.
Ha, ha.

PEPPER. (*Wipes off his face with his sleeve. Barely
controlling himself*) So now I'm going to play the fountain and you get the water.

ZACH. (*Still laughing*) You, the fountain?

PEPPPER. Yes, me.

ZACH. I get the water?

PEPPER. Yes, you.

ZACH. So be it. I get the water. (*He thrusts the bottle
into* PEPPER's *hand and takes a few paces. Thirsting for
revenge,* PEPPER *takes a huge swallow and stands waiting
with very bloated cheeks.* ZACHARIAS *stops without turn-
ing around.*) Pepper?

PEPPER. (*Hastily spits out the water*) What?

ZACH. (*Innocently*) Are you ready, Pepper?

PEPPER. Yes, Zacharias. (*He quickly takes another swallow*)

ZACH. Pepper?

PEPPER. (*Again spits the water out*) What?

ZACH. So it's okay for me to come.

PEPPER. Ye-e-es! (*Takes another swallow*)

ZACH. Pepper? (*At first, he gets no answer. Once again*) Pepper?

PEPPER. (*Spits*) What now?

ZACH. I'm coming. (PEPPER *quickly takes another swallow.* ZACHARIAS *approaches* PEPPER *and stops before him.* PEPPER *mumbles something incomprehensible with his mouth full*) What are you trying to say?

PEPPER. (*Spitting out the water. Angrily*) That's all wrong. You have to say it.

ZACH. What do I have to say?

PEPPER. (*Screaming*) That with the water. You know what I mean. You just want to spoil my turn. (*He is so furious that he is unaware that* ZACHARIAS *has taken the water bottle from him*)

ZACH. What do I have to say?

PEPPER. Please, water.

ZACH. Please, what? (*He turns aside and takes a big swallow*)

PEPPER. (*Very loud, very angry*) Please, water, please.

ZACHARIAS. (*Sprays water into* PEPPER's *face and bends over shaking with laughter*) Please, ho, ho, ha, ha, water, he, he, please, ho, ha. Fantastomatic. (*He sings.*)

> Please, water, please, please
> Look, look how on his knees
> He begs to be moister
> Than a wet, soggy oyster.

PEPPER, *highly incensed, yanks the bottle out of* ZACHARIAS' *hand and tries to pour the water over his head. The bottle is empty.* ZACHARIAS *has another attack of laughing.*

ZACHARIAS. It's empty. I've drunk it all. It's been a joke. A fantastomatic joke.

PEPPER. You're mean, really mean. I'm through being your friend.

ZACH. (*Stops laughing, almost threatening*) You're through being *my* friend?

PEPPER. Because you sprayed water all over me. (*Less sure of himself*)

ZACH. Through being *my* friend? (PEPPER *nods*) You mean to say, *I* am through being *your* friend. I don't want to have as friends people who can't take a joke and especially people with such a shabby box. (*He kicks* PEPPER's *box contemptuously*)

PEPPER. Don't touch my box. (ZACHARIAS *kicks the box forcefully a second time. In response,* PEPPER *runs over to* ZACHARIAS' *box and kicks it triumphantly. A bitter fight breaks out in which each kicks, shoves, scratches and spits at the other's box. Finally* PEPPER *hits* ZACHARIAS' *box very hard. He yells, jumps in pain in a circle and holds his foot.* ZACHARIAS *laughs uncontrollably*)

ZACH. (*Snorts*) He jumps around like a bull frog! Fantastomatic! (PEPPER *sticks out his tongue, climbs into his box and disappears entirely.* ZACHARIAS *goes to his own box, tries to turn it around but can't do it himself. He tries a number of times, gives up and ambles near* PEPPER's *box. Loud humming can be heard from it.* PEPPER *is imitating the sound of airplanes. Fascinated,* ZACHARIAS *steps closer*) Hey, Pepper (*No reply*) Pepper!

PEPPER. (*Raises his head beyond the edge suspiciously*) Yeh, what now?

ZACH. What are you doing in there?

PEPPER. I am playing airplane. (*He imitates an airplane motor and disappears again into the box*)

ZACH. That's not how it is. Airplanes have to have wings.

PEPPER. (*Rising again*) Wings?

ZACH. Yes, wings, like chickens and ducks.

PEPPER. My box doesn't have any wings.

ZACH. Then stick out your arms like this. (*He shows him how.* PEPPER *copies him and adds the sound of motors. Then* ZACHARIAS, *caught up in the game, begins to play airplane also*) Hey, Pepper.

PEPPER. What?

ZACH. Put your arms through the hole. That will make it look more real.

PEPPER. Through the holes of the handkerchief?

ZACH. You idiot, through the holes in the box. (PEPPER *sticks both hands through the holes. There appears on the* RIGHT *side a tiny arm, on the* LEFT *a giant one.* ZACHARIAS *screams in excitement*) Pepper! (*He points to the big arm*)

PEPPER. What's the matter?

ZACH. Your arm.

PEPPER. What about it?

ZACH. Huge like a giant. That's fantastomatic. Is the other one just as big? (*He runs to the other side of the box*) It's small, quite small. How do you do that? (PEPPER *pulls both arms out of the openings. He bends over the edge of the box and looks through the holes from outside in. Then he shrugs helplessly, glances suspiciously at* ZACHARIAS, *who is beside himself with excitement*) Stick your arms through the hole once again. Incomprehensible. And now the left. Unbelievable. (PEPPER *glances over the edge and only now sees his two changed arms. He is frightened and pulls the arms back quickly. Then he rises, feels his arms which are entirely normal. Hesitantly, he tries once again and again one arm becomes huge and the other tiny*)

PEPPER. (*With growing delight*) It doesn't hurt at all. Absolutely, first rate. It's fantastic. In fact, fantastomatic. That's what I call a box, eh? None other like it.

ZACH. It's crazy. I have to find out if it works with me. (*He is about to climb into* PEPPER's *box*)

PEPPER. Hey, out of my box. That would be just like you. First, to spit at my box, then to climb in.

ZACH. That was just kidding. I didn't even hit it. I spat *next* to it, like this. (*Demonstrates*)

PEPPER. I don't find anything funny in spitting.

ZACH. Don't be so touchy. Besides, I'm not doing it anymore. Besides, my mouth is completely dry. Look, nothing. (*He spits a number of times but nothing comes out*)

PEPPER. All the same, you did spit on my box.

ZACH. I'll wipe it off, Pepper. We don't want to fight

about a thing like that. (*He pulls out his handkerchief and wipes the box*) Was it here?

PEPPER. No, there. (*He points to a spot on the outside which* ZACHARIAS *wipes*. PEPPER *points to another spot, very far removed*) And there. (ZACHARIAS *wipes there also*)

ZACH. (*While he is wiping vigorously*) I like it that we're getting along again. You don't have to be afraid. I'm going to be your friend for good. That was just a joke that I said then.

PEPPER. Zacky?

ZACH. (*First wants to correct him but controls himself*) What?

PEPPER. Way down there. That's where you spat.

ZACH. (*Leans way down and wipes*) If you would like to have my box for a while, we can swap. I'll be glad to lend you mine, if you want it.

PEPPER. A box isn't a rental car.

ZACH. Well, just a suggestion. (*He keeps wiping*)

PEPPER. Zacky?

ZACH. What, Pepper?

PEPPER. I don't like your wearing your hat while you work.

ZACH. Should I take it off?

PEPPER. Yes, give it to me. (*Puts it on*)

ZACH. May I now get in?

PEPPER. Later, Zacky.

ZACH. Why later?

PEPPER. First, we're going to play.

ZACH. Play what?

PEPPER. You know all kinds of interesting games.

ZACH. We can play Aggravation.

PEPPER. Don't want to.

ZACH. Or Blind Man's Bluff.

PEPPER. Don't like it.

ZACH. Or Leap Frog.

PEPPER. Nothing doing.

ZACH. Concentration?

PEPPER. Out of the question.

ZACH. Heads and Tails?

PEPPER. Boring.

ZACH. Four Squares?

PEPPER. No good.

ZACH. Going to Jerusalem.

PEPPER. Uninteresting.

ZACH. Ghosts?

PEPPER. Dull.

ZACH. Red Rover.

PEPPER. Childish.

ZACH. We can sing.

PEPPER. Silly.

ZACH. You are right.

PEPPER. How do you mean I'm right?

ZACH. Singing is silly.

PEPPER. Says who?

ZACH. You.

PEPPER. You must have heard wrong. Let's sing together and loud.

ZACH. You don't even know how to sing.

PEPPER. And you?

ZACH. How can we both sing together loud if you don't know how to sing?

PEPPER. We sing together like this. You sing loud while I listen loud.

ZACH. That doesn't make sense.

PEPPER. (*Snitty*) Maybe not. (*He begins to play by himself. He reaches his arm through the hole in the box and says*) Bang! (*He pulls it back. Says*) Wham! (*Repeats several times*)

ZACH. Honestly, doesn't this hurt?

PEPPER. What?

ZACH. When your arm gets that large?

PEPPER. Can't feel it at all. Bang, wham, bang, wham.

ZACH. Hey, Pepper.

PEPPER. What?

ZACH. We can try it.

PEPPER. Try what?

ZACH. Well, singing.

PEPPER. Don't feel like it.

ZACH. Why not, Pepper. Singing is beautiful. (*He takes a few steps and sings, Ta, ra, ta, ta, then steps and looks expectantly toward* PEPPER)

PEPPER. Okay, start off.

ZACH. What should I sing?

PEPPER. Maybe a song.

ZACH. That's obvious but which?

PEPPER. A song with a box.

ZACH. A song with a box?

PEPPER. You heard me.

ZACH. There's no such thing.

PEPPER. Well, if there isn't, there isn't. (*He pushes his other arm through the other hole, saying wham, bang*)

ZACH. Pepper.

PEPPER. What?

ZACH. (*Hastily*) I'm going to make one up, especially for you.

PEPPER. Make up what?

ZACH. A song with a box. Wait, what rhymes with box? . . . A pair of sox are in a box.

PEPPER. I think this is super dumb. (*He resumes playing*)

ZACH. Wait a minute, wait a minute, I've got something new. How do you like this? I rocks my box.

PEPPER. You can rock your box as much as you like, but you're not going to rock mine.

ZACH. Here's a good one.

 We nest in our box

 Safe from the crow and the fox.

PEPPER. Ha, ha, we nest. I'm not a bird.

ZACH. (*Very angry*) No, you're not a bird, but you are coo-coo. You're super coo-coo. (*He jumps around the box, beats his arms as though they were wings and yells jeeringly*) Cock-a-doodle-doo.

PEPPER. (*Furious, he throws his hat at* ZACHARIAS) You're not going to get into my box, even if you stand on your blockhead.

ZACH. What would I do in your silly box? It stinks like a monkey house.

PEPPER. Monkeys don't have houses.

ZACH. Well, what do they have?

PEPPER. Fleas.

ZACH. Then it stinks like a smelly cheese.

PEPPER. Not true.
ZACH. Is.
PEPPER. Isn't.
ZACH. Is.
PEPPER. No.
ZACH. Yes it does, yes it does.

While they are arguing the DRUM MAJOR *appears. He has a marching drum slung over his shoulder with cymbals attached to the top. He beats a catchy marching tune and sings with it. He marches past both of them without giving them a glance. Before they have recovered from their surprise, he has disappeared.* PEPPER *climbs out of his box and stares after him.*

PEPPER. Did you see that? Did you see that? That's how he marched. (*He marches in an exaggerated way*) Rum ta ta rum ta ta. (ZACHARIAS *trips him,* PEPPER *falls on his belly.* ZACHARIAS *yells at* PEPPER *on the ground*)

ZACH. Rum ta ta. And it's your fault that he went off. Why didn't you talk to him?

PEPPER. Why should I talk to him. You're fatter.

ZACH. I'm fatter? Very funny.

PEPPER. We can measure that.

ZACH. By all means let us. (*He takes off his coat, measures his coat, measures his waist with his hand and shows the distance*) That's how thin I am. (*Then he walks over to* PEPPER, *puts one hand on his shoes and extends the other to his head. He shows with extended arms*) That's how fat you are.

PEPPER. Ha! You cheated.

ZACH. *I* cheated?

PEPPER. Of course. You first took off your coat. (*He also removes his coat*) So I am also thin.

At this moment, the DRUM MAJOR *reappears. As before, he marches past the two, clear across the stage. Immediately after that he disappears. The two quickly put on their coats.*

ZACH. (*Whispering the whole time*) Go on, speak to
him. Go on, say something. Hurry. Speak to him. (*He
kicks him*) Now he's gone. You oaf.

PEPPER. (*Crying*) You're always bawling me out. I
don't have any idea how to speak to him.

ZACH. All right. We'll practice. (*He grabs* PEPPER *by
his shoulders and places him in front of himself. He
steps back a few paces. He assumes a new demeanor,
raises one finger and begins to imitate the* DRUM MAJOR
as he marches off with a rum ta ta. PEPPER *runs after
him and marches alongside delighted.* ZACHARIAS, un-
*nerved, makes a face, stops and puts his hand on his
waist.* PEPPER *bumps into him and continues to march
in place*)

ZACH. (*Yells at him*) You're supposed to address me.

PEPPER. What am I supposed to say?

ZACH. Good morning, my name is Pepper.

PEPPER. Ha ha. Your name is Zacharias.

ZACH. (*Kicks him*) But your name is Pepper. You
hippo!

For the third time, the DRUM MAJOR *appears.* PEPPER
and ZACHARIAS *shove each other in his direction.
Neither dares to address him. Each pushes the other
ahead. As the* DRUM MAJOR *is about to go off,*
ZACHARIAS *pulls himself together and stands deter-
mined in his path. He bows very low and remains
there for a long time. The* DRUM MAJOR *stops and
ceases to play.* ZACHARIAS *continues to bow.*

ZACH. (*Bent over*) Good morning.

MAJOR. (*Very curt*) Morning.

ZACH. (*Still bent over*) Pepper wants to address you.

PEPPER. (*Whispering*) Speak to him.

ZACH. (*Raising himself*) What did you say?

PEPPER. Talk to him.

ZACH. (*Bending down again*) Pepper wants to talk to
you.

MAJOR. Well, then.

ZACH. (*Stands up, pushes* PEPPER *before him, pushes*
PEPPER's *head down for a bow*) Go on, say something.

PEPPER. Like this, I can't talk.

ZACH. What do you mean like this?

PEPPER. With the head down.

ZACH. But you are talking.

PEPPER. (*Resentfully*) Good morning, my name is Pepper.

MAJOR. So much I know.

PEPPER. (*Straightens up and looks delighted at* ZACHARIAS) He knows me. (*He turns to the* DRUM MAJOR *and points to* ZACHARIAS) Do you know him too?

MAJOR. No.

PEPPER. He doesn't know you. That's Zacky.

ZACH. Zach-a-ri-asss!

PEPPER. We think it's nice the way you walk around, really nice, with ram tam tam. (*He starts to march*)

ZACH. It's fantastomatic.

PEPPER. And that's a fine drum. Drums real nice. Ram ta ta ta. (*He imitates the march and infects* ZACHARIAS *with it. Both march in a circle around the* DRUM MAJOR)

MAJOR. (*Hits the cymbals and shouts*) Quiet! Number one, that's not walking, that's marching. Number two, that's not an ordinary drum, that's a marching drum. Third, it makes me sick to look at you. That's how badly you march.

PEPPER. So show us how you munch.

MAJOR. *March!*

PEPPER. May we also hit the drum?

ZACH. And also the metal thing up there? Ping, ping, ping.

MAJOR. (*Hits the cymbals and shouts*) Quiet! First we will march, then you may hit the drum once.

ZACH. Fantastomatic.

PEPPER. Really, super terrific.

MAJOR. Quiet! No talking in-between. All in step!

PEPPER. (*Puzzled*) What are we supposed to step on?

ZACH. Don't know. On all he said.

PEPPER. You can't step on all.

ZACH. Then step a little bit. Go on before he starts yelling again. (*He pushes him with his elbow.* PEPPER *raises his foot uncertainly several times. Then both*

stand and look at the DRUM MAJOR *in order to discover
what he could have meant*)

MAJOR. (*Shouting*) Line up!

ZACH. Oh, well.

PEPPER. You see. (*Neither makes a move*)

MAJOR. What's the matter. I'm waiting.

ZACH. There is no line.

PEPPER. Nowhere.

MAJOR. One stand behind the other.

PEPPER. Oh, well.

ZACH. Why didn't he say that? (PEPPER *takes a position in front of* ZACHARIAS)

ZACH. Hey, he said behind the other. You're standing
in front of me.

PEPPER. Excuse me. (*He now goes behind* ZACHARIAS)
Now you're standing in front of me. Now you have to
stand behind me.

ZACH. I stay where I stay!

PEPPER. As you like. (*He steps again in front of*
ZACHARIAS)

ZACH. Will you please go behind me, you wise guy. I
am marching first.

PEPPER. That's what you think.

ZACH. We'll see about that. (*He stands now in front of*
PEPPER) You think you can march first because you've
got two holes in your box.

PEPPER. You're jealous. Because you can't make things
big and small with your box.

ZACH. Big and small, big and small. My box is seventeen times better than yours.

PEPPER. Better? (*He turns to the* DRUM MAJOR *who
has been listening impatiently*) Come, I'll show you my
box.

MAJOR. Now we'll march.

ZACH. No. My box. Come here to my box. Pepper, here,
let's turn my box around. (PEPPER *turns his back to
him*)

MAJOR. Go on, help him. So we can finally do our
marching. (PEPPER *and* ZACHARIAS *turn the box over
twice*)

ZACH. Isn't this a magic box? You see it's green and now watch it. Red. Big time, eh? Fantastomatic.

MAJOR. (*Genuinely surprised*) Amazing. Changes color as it's turned.

ZACH. Now I'll show you Pepper's box. You'll be amazed again. (*He prepares to climb into* PEPPER's *box*)

PEPPER. Leave my box alone. (*He pulls* ZACHARIAS *away and climbs in himself*) Now watch. (*He pushes the two different-sized arms out of the box*) Wham, bang, wham, bang.

MAJOR. I'll be damned!

PEPPER. Bang, wham, bang, wham.

MAJOR. Extraordinary, remarkable! The most remarkable boxes I've ever come across.

ZACH. Which do you like best? Mine?

PEPPER. Mine, of course.

MAJOR. I like them both. Yes, both. (*He nods approvingly at both boxes*)

ZACH. Who can march first?

MAJOR. What did you say? Oh, yes, marching. Let me think. Best thing is for each of you to practice by yourself. More likely to succeed that way. (*He hangs the drum around* ZACHARIAS' *neck and gives him the drum sticks*) Hit the drums and forward march. One, two, one, two. (*He pushes* ZACHARIAS OFF STAGE *and shouts after him*) Practice well and no stopping even after three hundred paces!

PEPPER. You let him march and you let him hit the drum.

MAJOR. (*Putting his hand on* PEPPER's *shoulder*) Leave him, you'll get your turn. Then the drum is going to sound much louder.

PEPPER. Much louder?

MAJOR. Of course, much louder. It's got to be warmed up or else I wouldn't have first sent Fatso off.

PEPPER. Who?

MAJOR. The fat one. Can't stand him, can you, that showoff? (PEPPER *is about to gently contradict him but the* DRUM MAJOR *doesn't give him a chance*) I get it, I get it only too well. A disgusting big talker. The way he treats you, really mean.

PEPPER. It's a fact. He never lets me shorten his name. He always says Zacharias.

MAJOR. You see, you see. He surely never lets you into his box, this Zacky. (PEPPER *shakes his head self-pityingly*) I could see that at first glance, the kind of guy he is. His box isn't much. Not much at all.

PEPPER. He always calls me animal names.

MAJOR. Animal names. Devilish. What a pig! I could see right away what you thought when he marched off.

PEPPER. (*Surprised*) I?

MAJOR. You are right, absolutely right. He's got to be taught a lesson. We have to take something from him that he really likes.

PEPPER. How about his hat? He's always got it on, even when he sleeps.

MAJOR. Right. His hat, for example. But that we can't take away because he isn't here. What could we take away? (*Looks around, nothing occurs to him. He shrugs*) If only he'd left something behind.

PEPPER. Only the box.

MAJOR. Right! This man can think, splendid. We'll take his box away from him. I'll make you my head-marcher. You may march behind me, immediately behind me. But not a word to Fatso. Okay? Now grab hold of the box.

PEPPER. But that isn't right. What's Zacky going to say?

MAJOR. You're not going to be a spoilsport, you're not going to be chicken? After all, it was your idea. Are you afraid?

PEPPER. What are you going to do with the box?

MAJOR. My truck is over there. A good hiding place. Grab hold of it.

PEPPER. What if Zacky is going to be angry.

MAJOR. Why should he be angry with you? He doesn't know that you've hidden his box.

PEPPER. But then we'll give it back to him. All right? (*In the meantime, the drumbeats have become louder.* ZACHARIAS *is returning*)

MAJOR. The elephant walrus is coming back. What are we going to do with the box? After all, yours is the bigger. Let's put his into yours. Quick, on the double. (*They put* ZACHARIAS' *box into* PEPPER's) Not a word to Zacky. That's agreed. Best thing is—you be gone. Or else he'd be able to tell by your face. Don't look so dumb, Mr. Headmarcher. It's only a joke. You want to be part of a joke, don't you? (*They just manage to hide the box.* ZACHARIAS *returns marching. He proudly keeps banging the drums and the cymbal. He's marking time in order to show* PEPPER *how it's done*)

ZACH. Surprised, eh? This is the right article. Fantastomatic.

MAJOR. Very expert. (*He removes the drum from him and puts it on* PEPPER) All right, now it's your turn. Pay attention to the beat. One, two, one, two, and so on.

ZACH. (*The expert*) He's hitting it too fast. Much too excited. Slower, Pepper. More feeling. He just doesn't have the gift. (PEPPER *is off*)

MAJOR. Could be a fact. Doesn't compare to you.

ZACH. Really?

MAJOR. Can't get it through my head, how you can have a friend like that. With your talents. That dwarf, he isn't all there, is he?

ZACH. Well, now . . .

MAJOR. Not much of a friendship, I'm sure. More like acquaintances, I guess.

ZACH. Well . . .

MAJOR. Nor do I understand how a flea like him ever got a box like that. His is far superior to yours.

ZACH. That's not true. Mine . . . (*He realizes only now that his box is gone*) My box! My box is gone. My box, where's my box?

MAJOR. Your box. You must be kidding.

ZACH. (*Looking everywhere*) Somebody has swiped my box. It's been stolen. Didn't you see who took it? My box is gone.

MAJOR. Didn't see a thing. I've been listening to you. Still I have certain ideas . . . If I were you, I'd put a few questions to your friend.

ZACH. Pepper? I'm going to clobber him if he did it. I'm going to get him.

MAJOR. And if he doesn't admit it? You've got to be smarter than that.

ZACH. So what shall I do?

MAJOR. You've got to force it. Put it to him this way: either you give me back my box or . . .

ZACH. Or?

MAJOR. I keep something of yours.

ZACH. Indeed, keep what?

MAJOR. Hmm, keep what?

ZACH. I don't have anything of his.

MAJOR. Then take something. Look around.

ZACH. I don't see anything.

MAJOR. And what is that?

ZACH. The box?!

MAJOR. That's it. Took you a good long time. You take my box, I'll take your box. That's clear and simple.

ZACH. Maybe it wasn't even Pepper.

MAJOR. Entirely unimportant. He's got to be taught a lesson. Such a wise guy and he keeps insisting that his box is better than yours. Marches like an orangutan and pretends to be a headmarcher.

ZACH. Is that true?

MAJOR. That's what he said. But he's in for a surprise. I've thought of someone else for that job. Got my meaning? Of course, this is strictly between you and me. We'll hide the box, over there on my truck. You may march directly behind me but it has to remain a secret as we said. He can keep looking for it for a long time, eh? That'll be a killer of a joke. Just imagine his dumb face. Attention! Pu-u-sh, push. Easy does it.

ZACH. (*Pushing against the box*) It's good and heavy.

MAJOR. No problem for experienced marchers. Keep shoving.

Slowly they push the box OFFSTAGE. *A few seconds later* PEPPER *marching proudly returns. With the cymbal he strikes the drum and with the drumsticks he strikes the cymbal. He walks in a large circle on the stage. He hasn't realized that he is alone.*

PEPPER. (*Over his shoulder*) Hey, Zacky, you haven't

said a thing. Flabbergasted, eh? Great, eh? Bang, bang, ta ra. (*He turns around*) Zacky, Zach-a-ri-asss. The box is gone. I'm all alone in the world. Zacharias! The box!

> ZACHARIAS *and* DRUM MAJOR *return.* ZACHARIAS *tries to hide a little behind the* DRUM MAJOR *and looks at* PEPPER *anxiously.*

PEPPER. My box is gone too! Someone has taken my box!

MAJOR. Has to be investigated. Carefully investigated. Look at yourself. Did you use that to hit the drum? (*He takes the cymbal from him*) Go on, hit it! (PEPPER *listlessly strikes the cymbal with the drum stick*)

MAJOR. Incredible! About time that you march properly. Let me have it. (*He straps the drum on himself*) Pepper, you march first. You like that, eh?

PEPPER. Nothing matters to me if I don't have my box.

MAJOR. Forget your box. That'll be carefully investigated. Right now let Fatty go first. Are you ready? When I say forward march, you march off. It's always one, two, begin with the left foot. Which is your left foot? (PEPPER *points unenthusiastically to his left arm.* ZACHARIAS *points eagerly to his right foot*)

MAJOR. (*Steps on the left foot of each*) That's the left foot. That's the one you start with. Forward, march. One, two, one, two, rum, rum ta ta. That's right, first class. Doing it right. (PEPPER *and* ZACHARIAS *march in a circle across the stage.* PEPPER *is at first indifferent, but with praise from the* DRUM MAJOR *marches spiritedly. The* DRUM MAJOR *withdraws unnoticed from the stage. His praises and commands are still heard as he moves further and further away.* PEPPER *and* ZACHARIAS *fall out of step, then one can hear a truck starting and driving off in high gear.* PEPPER *and* ZACHARIAS *run to the edge of the stage*)

ZACH. He's driving away.

PEPPER. Simply driving away.

ZACH. Such a dog!

PEPPER. What a meany!

ZACH. Such an ape! Such a hippo! Such a beast. I'll kick him in the behind if I ever get hold of him again.

PEPPER. He was no friend. He just pretended.

(Brief silence)

ZACH. Hey, Pepper.

PEPPER. What.

ZACH. I have to tell you something.

PEPPER. What?

ZACH. You . . . your box . . .

PEPPER. What about my box?

ZACH. It's in his truck. *(Hurriedly)* I just wanted to hide it. I would have returned it to you. Right away. He said you had to be taught a lesson. So I helped him . . .

PEPPER. You helped him?! A fine friend you turned out to be. The hell with you. *(He spits in front of him)* I would never have believed it.

ZACH. I'm very sorry.

PEPPER. Sorry, sorry! That doesn't help me a bit. *(Pause.)* Zacky!

ZACH. *(Very sad)* Zach-a-ri-ass.

PEPPER. Zachariass, I have to tell you something.

ZACH. Go on.

PEPPER. Something bad about your box.

ZACH. *(Grabbing hold of him)* My box? What have you done with it?

PEPPER. He put it into mine.

ZACH. In yours?

PEPPER. He said it was just a joke. I meant to give it back to you. Right away. But how can I take it out if my box is gone too?

ZACH. You helped him. You worm.

PEPPER. Just a bit. He said you had to be taught a lesson. He turned me against you. *(ZACHARIAS shakes him furiously until PEPPER cries)* If you hadn't carried off my box, yours would still be here too.

ZACH. *(Letting him go)* You're right. He cheated both of us, the liar.

PEPPER. He said he was going to make me the headmarcher.

ZACH. You abandoned your friend, Zacharias, just so you could become a headmarcher.

PEPPER. You also wanted to march first. And besides you wanted to teach me a lesson too. You just said so.

ZACH. You, me, too. We're beginning to argue again. Everything that happened, happened because we didn't stick together.

PEPPER. It's our fault.

ZACH. We made it very easy for him. All he does is promise you something and right away you cheat your friend Zacharias.

PEPPER. And you your friend Pepper.

ZACH. It's our fault. (*They sadly sit down where their boxes formerly stood*)

PEPPER *begins to do gymnastic exercises.* ZACHARIAS *takes out his toothbrush and brushes his hair and shoes.*

PEPPER. You're all right. At least, you still have a carton and a toothbrush.

ZACH. You still have a bottle.

PEPPER. It's empty.

ZACH. My carton, too. (*He listlessly keeps on brushing*) I once knew someone who could blow on a bottle like a steamboat's whistle.

PEPPER. On a bottle?

ZACH. Yes, like this. (*He tries it but all that comes out is a sad hissing*)

PEPPER. Let me try. (*He tries without success. In the meantime,* ZACHARIAS *examines his carton*)

ZACH. Looks actually like a truck. You just have to imagine the headlights. And the wheels. (ZACHARIAS *has stood up and pushes the carton along the ground. There is a rattling noise. Surprised, he stops. At that very moment, the noise stops too. He pushes it a little further and again there is a noise.* PEPPER *gets up and watches fascinated.* ZACHARIAS *pushes the box across the stage, behind the backdrop. When he reappears on the other side of the backdrop, the clatter has become louder and the carton bigger*)

PEPPER. Hey, Zacharias, look!

ZACH. (*The noise ceases*) What's the matter?

PEPPER. Your carton got bigger.
ZACH. Really?
PEPPER. Drive it around once more.

ZACHARIAS *pushes the little box several times at increasing speed around the backdrop. Every time he reappears, the clatter becomes louder and the box larger. At last the box is as large as the old one. Exhausted,* ZACHARIAS *stops* CENTER STAGE.

ZACH. Pfgh. No more driving around. The carton has gotten too heavy. (*He wipes the sweat off*)
PEPPER. What do you mean carton? This is an honest-to-goodness box. Just as big as the one that he swiped.
ZACH. (*Realizes it only now*) Box! Man that's crazy, fantastomatic. (*He walks around the box, steps inside*)
PEPPER. Hey, Zacharias.
ZACH. Absolutely first rate. Nice box, nice box.
PEPPER. Zacharias, that's our box isn't it? I mean it belongs to both of us. Doesn't it?
ZACH. Both of us? You've got to be batty.
PEPPER. But you'll lend it to me.
ZACH. (*Polishing the edge of the box*) A box is not a rental car.
PEPPER. May I climb in just once?
ZACH. With those dirty feet?
PEPPER. If you don't let me in, I'm not going to be your friend anymore. (ZACHARIAS *continues to polish his box*) I'm going to find myself another friend.
ZACH. Without a box?

PEPPER *turns around and walks away angrily.* ZACHARIAS *doesn't notice that* PEPPER *has disappeared. After a while, he looks up and realizes that he is all alone.*

ZACH. (*Astonished*) Pepper?

ZACHARIAS *shrugs and keeps on cleaning his box but soon he loses interest and, annoyed, throws down his handkerchief. He stands inside the box and considers intently what he should do next. Then he climbs out of the box and tries to turn it around. But by himself, he can't do it. He furiously kicks the box and climbs back in. Now he begins to play airplane. It's no fun. His arms keep dropping lower and finally he cries out, "PEPPER." No reply. ZACHARIAS climbs out of the box and starts looking for PEPPER. Unsuccessful, he sits down in front of the box in complete despair. At that moment, PEPPER returns because he has forgotten his bottle. He stumbles over ZACHARIAS.*

PEPPER. What's the matter with you?

ZACH. You left me alone.

PEPPER. Left you alone, left you alone! This box was more important to you than a friend.

ZACH. It was only a joke, Pepper. This box belongs to both of us. We found out together how to make it bigger.

PEPPER. Now you tell me. But later you're going to say it's your box and kick me out.

ZACH. Never again. It's much too boring in that box alone. Come get in. It belongs to both of us.

PEPPER. Okay. (*He climbs into the box and helps* ZACHARIAS *when he gets in*) Wait I'll help you. A great box, our box. Really super, extra super. And so cozy.

ZACH. Before you said it was worm-eaten.

PEPPER. I was just kidding, because you annoyed me. This box is okay. Perfect for playing airplane. Really phenomenal.

ZACH. Phenomenal?

PEPPER. Yes, terrific. Or maybe it could be a motorcycle with a passenger seat on the side. One of us can sit on the edge like a side-car passenger. (ZACHARIAS *makes loud motor sounds and* PEPPER *joins in excitedly*)

ZACH. Watch it. Curve! (*He sits on the edge of the box*) Lean over! (*He leans out so far that he almost falls out of the box.* PEPPER *pulls him back in*) Fantastomatic.

PEPPER. You can do this only if there are two of us. If there are two of us, playing in a box is better. Hey, we can also play police car. Fa too ta too ta. Listen there's a song for a box. I just didn't tell you before.

ZACH. What's it called?

PEPPER. Seven cops. That goes well with a police car.

ZACH. I know it.

PEPPER. Why didn't you sing it then?

ZACH. Because it's about cops.

PEPPER. And about boxes. (*He starts to sing and* ZACHARIAS *sings along*)

> Seven thick, fat copses
> Who weighed almost a ton
> Fell into some boxes
> One by one by one.
> Their sergeant wrote a letter
> To the Chief Justice of the state
> To send slim men, maybe eight.

While they are still singing, one can hear drumbeats. The DRUM MAJOR *returns. He is wearing a different hat and a false nose. It's impossible to tell whether he is the former one returning disguised or another* DRUM MAJOR. *Again he marches arrogantly across the stage. This time however the two are so deeply absorbed in their games that they don't notice him. Unsuccessfully, he tries to get their attention. Then he speaks to them.*

MAJOR. Well, you two. Don't want to march with me. One, two, one, two. Hut, hup, eh?

ZACH. Don't feel like it.

PEPPER. We're playing.

ZACH. Racing car, drrr, drr, drrm. (PEPPER *joins him in making racing car sounds*)

MAJOR. Racing car? Ridiculous.

PEPPER. We like it.

MAJOR. (*To* ZACHARIAS) That shrimp's got a pretty big mouth. You're putting up with that?

ZACH. If that bothers you, you don't have to listen.

PEPPER. (*Triumphant*) If you want to go, nobody's stopping you.

MAJOR. And that's what I'm going to do. . . . But seriously, a little marching would be good for both of you. Especially that fat gentleman. Then you'd have a little more room in the box, eh? (*He laughs loudly*)

PEPPER. (*Cool*) We've got enough room.

ZACH. Better fat than dumb.

MAJOR. All kinds of fancy ideas with your ratty box. Racing car and such. You're too stupid to learn how to march properly. Yep, that's it. You're childish. Racing car! (*He goes off furious*)

ZACH. Beat it. Or we're going to help you out of here. (*Raises his arm threateningly*)

PEPPER. Yes, on the double, one, two, one, two, you kangaroo. I gave it to him.

ZACH. We showed him. Fantabulous. What are we going to play now?

PEPPER. We'll sing.

ZACH. And what will we sing?

PEPPER. The second part.

ZACH. The second part is fine. Who starts off?

PEPPER. Both of us.

ZACH. Both of us. Right. (*They sing the second stanza together. As they sing, they slowly sink into the box. At the very end, they raise their heads one last time. Then they disappear for good*)

> Seven thick, fat copses
> Who weighed almost a ton
> Climbed out of the boxes
> One by one by one.
> The sergeant burnt the letter
> Which he didn't have to send.
> It turned out for the better,
> Which brings us to the end . . .

—THE END—

MUSIC USE NOTE

Licensees are solely responsible for obtaining formal written permission from copyright owners to use copyrighted music in the performance of this play and are strongly cautioned to do so. If no such permission is obtained by the licensee, then the licensee must use only original music that the licensee owns and controls. Licensees are solely responsible and liable for all music clearances and shall indemnify the copyright owners of the play(s) and their licensing agent, Samuel French, against any costs, expenses, losses and liabilities arising from the use of music by licensees. Please contact the appropriate music licensing authority in your territory for the rights to any incidental music.

IMPORTANT BILLING AND CREDIT REQUIREMENTS

If you have obtained performance rights to this title, please refer to your licensing agreement for important billing and credit requirements.